Friends of the
MENEHUNES

This book is dedicated to my parents, Norma Lei Noland and
Joseph Royce Noland, for all of their love and support throughout my life.

Book Orders and Inquiries:

Kaukini Ranch Press
P.O. Box 2462
Wailuku, Hawaii 96793

First Published in September 1994 by Kaukini Ranch Press
Second Printing September, 1996

Library of Congress Catalog Number 94-96609
ISBN: 0-9643674-0-8

Copyright © 1994 Kaukini Ranch Press
Printed in Hong Kong

Friends of the
MENEHUNES

written and illustrated by:
Karen Lei Noland

Kaukini Ranch Press
Kahakuloa, Maui, Hawaii

Once upon a time, on the island of Oahu, there lived a very special family. There was a mother, a father, a girl named Mele and a boy named Moki. They were menehunes, the tiny elf-like people of Hawaii. Menehunes are wonderful builders and very hard workers. They live in the lush rain forests of the mountains.

Menehunes work at night while everyone else is sleeping. When the moon is high in the sky they come out to work and to play. During the day they sleep and rest. Menehunes must be safe at home in their mountain forests before the early morning rooster crows.

One evening when Mama and Papa menehune were out working, Mele and Moki sat staring down at the big city lights below them.

Mele sighed, "How beautiful the lights are Moki. I wish we could go down just once to see the big city."

"Mele you know that is forbidden!" cried Moki.

"I know," sighed Mele, as she continued to stare dreamily down the valley.

"Come on Mele, let's go play your favorite game. Please.....I promise to let you go first!" cheered Moki.

Mele smiled and her eyes sparkled! "Oh yes Moki....Let's go," she cried as they ran to the top of the nearest small hill.

Moki grabbed a large ti leaf and waved it gleefully in the air. "Mele look...it's perfect!" he said. Mele carefully positioned herself in the middle of the ti leaf and Moki pushed her with all of his might. Whoooooshshshsh... Mele sailed down the hill in a rush of wind. Her tinkling laughter echoed in the night as the wind carried her voice high into the sky and into the valley below them.

Down in the valley below them lived another family. They too had a mother, a father and two children. The children's names were Anna and Joseph. This family was large, no menehunes here!
Anna and Joseph were just getting ready for bed. The night was warm, so Joseph opened up the window to let in a cool breeze.

Both children fluffed their pillows and tucked themselves in for the night when all of a sudden Anna heard a noise and sat straight up in the bed!

"What was that?" she cried!

The wind had carried the menehunes' laughter straight down to the valley below! It floated into the room on a breeze carrying the scent of plumeria blossoms.

"Ummmm," said Anna. "It must be the angels singing in heaven."

Joseph had also heard the noise.
"That's not singing...that's laughter. Someone is up on that mountain laughing!" he said.
"Ohhhh....I wonder who it is, said Anna. "Can we go look... please?"
"Not tonight, it's dark, maybe in the morning if we get an early start. It's a long way to the top of the mountain," yawned Joseph.
"HOORAY!" yelled Anna excitedly.
Soon they both fell fast asleep dreaming of the morning to come.

Finally morning came, and Anna and Joseph were up bright and early. They packed themselves a simple lunch of shrimp and poi. They wrapped their lunch in a large cloth and tied it to the end of a stick. Then they went outside to tell their father goodbye.

Their father was hard at work on a fishpond that he was building for their mother. He was sweating in the hot morning sun.

"Whew...this is hard work, and I am running out of stones for building," said father. "Where are you two headed so early?"

"We are going on a hike," said Joseph.

"That sounds like fun!" said Papa. "Don't go too far and be home early," he said.

"We will," they cried in unison as they headed down the street on their journey.

Joseph and Anna were soon in the dark forests of the
mountain.
On and on they walked, climbing higher and higher.
"Oh Joseph....how exciting. We are finally on our way to find the
laughing strangers," said Anna as she merrily skipped along.

The children had been hiking for some time now, and Joseph
was afraid Anna was getting tired.
"Anna, are you hungry? Would you like to rest and have lunch?"
said Joseph.
"No, let's go all the way to the top first," said Anna as they hiked
further and further up the mountain.

Pretty soon the sun started to dip into the sky. Joseph and
Anna had been so busy climbing that they hadn't realized that
soon it would be dark. Finally they had made it to the top of the
ridge. Exhausted, they both sat down on a nearby rock.

"I'm tired," sobbed Anna. "It's getting dark and we've only now reached the top. Mama and Papa will be worried about us. I'M SCARED."

Joseph was getting worried himself. The time had flown by so quickly.

"How are we going to get down the mountain before nightfall?" said Anna nervously.

"Don't worry," said Joseph. "I will take care of you."

Joseph was no longer eager to find the owners of the laughing voices. He quickly spread out the meal they had prepared earlier. Together he and Anna started their dinner as the sun sank lower and lower into the sky.

It was completely dark now, and the children could see the city lights below.

"Everything looks so tiny from up here," said Anna as she huddled closer to Joseph.

The wind started to howl between the trees, and an owl hooted in the distance.

"Oh Joseph...what shall we do?" said Anna as she started to cry.

Joseph put on a brave face and told Anna, "Why this is an adventure. We shall stay the night here and go down the mountain first thing in the morning. We will be fine, " he said, smiling assuredly at his little sister.

Anna managed a weak smile back, and soon the tired children were fast asleep.

Meanwhile, the two menehune children, Mele and Moki, were just waking from a deep sleep. They both stretched lazily as they slowly opened their eyes.
"Mele," said Moki, "Let's hurry with our chores so we can go and play our favorite game again."
Both menehunes got out of bed and quickly dressed themselves.

Mama and Papa menehune had already left for work. They were very busy for Papa was the chief of all the menehunes on the island of Oahu. His clan was very small now with only a few hundred members. Most of the menehunes had moved to the surrounding islands. The lights from the valley were getting closer and closer up the mountain every year, and the menehunes were running out of places to live.

Mele and Moki finished their daily chores and left to find the perfect ti leaf. They searched everywhere. Finally Mele spied the corner of a big ti leaf on the ground beside a large rock. She ran to the rock and was surprised by what she found.

Mele stared in disbelief at the two sleeping children.
"Oh my," she whispered.
Moki soon reached Mele, and he too was startled.
"Oh my goodness...I've never seen such big menehunes before,"
he said.
"Moki they are not menehunes...I think they are from the City of
Lights in the valley below," said Mele quietly.
"Look!" said Moki, "They have shrimp and poi!"
This particular meal was the menehunes favorite food. It was
very hard to come by .
Moki picked up the leftover food, and he and Mele began to eat
the remains of Anna and Joseph's dinner.

Moki and Mele were making such loud lip-smacking noises that they awoke the two sleeping children.

"Who are you?" said Joseph.

"Who are you, and why are you here?" demanded Moki, stretching to his full height of two feet.

"My name is Joseph, and this is my sister Anna," he said. "We live in the valley below you."

"You are so small," said Anna "Are you a menehune?"

"I am," said Moki proudly. "My name is Moki, and this is my sister Mele."

"Wow," said Joseph. "Was that you we heard laughing up there last night?"

"That was me," cried Mele! "We were playing our favorite game. Do you want to play?"

Moki and Mele explained the game to the two children and soon they were all laughing loudly as they took turns sliding down the hill on the ti leaf. Finally, after much playing, the children and the menehunes sat and rested.

"Maybe you and Mele can come down to the valley with us and go swimming at the beach one day," said Joseph to Moki.

"We aren't allowed," said Moki. "Our parent's won't let us. We are too small. Only the workers are allowed to go when they have work to do," he said.

"Our papa told us we must be careful not to be seen," said Mele. "We are a very quiet people and we do not want our homes to be disturbed," she said teasingly as she mimicked her father, the chief.

"What was that?" said Mele. "Was that the hoot of an owl?"
"Why yes," said Joseph. "He was flying around earlier this evening."
"OH NO!!!" screamed Mele. "RUN FOR THE HOUSE!!!"
Mele and Moki made a mad dash for the house as the two children looked on in confusion.

Joseph and Anna did not know that the owl was the menehunes' worst enemy. Both are night prowlers, and the owl is famous for catching his prey.

The owl hovered and swooped over the small menehunes' heads. Its great claws grabbed a hold of Mele's clothing and started to lift her into the air. Joseph managed to grab a hold of her feet just before the owl had lifted her out of reach. He hung on with all of his might as the owl struggled to lift his now heavy burden.

WHAM! The two captives fell to the ground with a loud thud. Mele and Joseph scrambled to their feet, and they all four ran for cover in the small house.

Moki slammed the door behind them. "Joseph, you saved my sister's life!" he said, as they all hugged and rejoiced. "Mele and I are going to lead you down the secret mountain path to your home in the valley below to help repay you for your bravery," said Moki.

The group headed downhill with torches to light the way. They walked endlessly into the night. Finally right before daybreak they came to the edge of the forest at the bottom of the mountain. Joseph and Anna promised to keep their menehune friends a secret. They all hugged and said their goodbyes. As Joseph and Anna turned to wave goodbye again, the early morning rooster crowed. The menehunes had already vanished.

Joseph and Anna ran the rest of the way home. When they arrived they found their worried parents waiting for them with outstretched arms.

They were hungry and tired and glad to be home. Everything was the same even the unfinished fishpond in the back.

That night, before the two children went to bed, they thought about their two new friends. They wondered when they would see them again before they drifted off to sleep.

Late after midnight, while the children were sleeping, there appeared many lights at the edge of the forest. The lights were torches carried by the menehunes. The chief had come with his many workers to repay Joseph and Anna for saving his daughter's life. The menehunes lined up and passed stones from a nearby stream to one another. They started to finish building the fishpond that Joseph and Anna's father had worked so hard on. They were swift and thorough with their job. By the time the morning rooster had crowed, all of the work was finished, and the menehunes had vanished into the mountain forests.

Joseph and Anna awoke when the rooster crowed. They ran outside to greet the day. In the yard they were amazed to find a fishpond with waterfalls and big Koi goldfish. Smack in the middle of that fishpond was a stone statue of a beautiful menehune maiden.

Joseph and Anna looked at one another and smiled. The menehunes had come in the night and finished their father's fishpond. They had wished to repay the children for saving Mele's life. Anna and Joseph looked to the top of the mountains and there they saw a magnificent rainbow framing the highest peak! They knew their newfound friends were up there somewhere, and they dreamed of the day they would meet again.